SOCCER CHAMPIONS

BY JIM WHITING

AC MILAN

CREATIVE EDUCATION • CREATIVE PAPERBACKS

Published by Creative Education
and Creative Paperbacks
P.O. Box 227, Mankato, Minnesota 56002
Creative Education and Creative Paperbacks
are imprints of The Creative Company
www.thecreativecompany.us

Design and production by The Design Lab
Art direction by Rita Marshall
Printed in Malaysia

Photographs by Corbis (Maurizio Borsari/AFLO/
Nippon News, Colorsport, Pierpaolo Ferreri, Marc
Francotte/TempSport, ALESSANDRO GAROFALO/
Reuters, Christian Liewig, Christian Liewig/TempSport,
Reuters, Sampics, Giampiero Sposito/Reuters),
Getty Images (Shaun Botterill, EyeOn, Bob Thomas),
photosinbox.com, Shutterstock (Albo, gualtiero boffi,
Paolo Bona, Boris15, Denis Kuvaev, Maxisport, Neftali,
Matt Trommer, ValeStock), Wikimedia Creative Commons
(Fra90Snake, Froztbyte/www.mysona.dk, Ganuh, José
Luiz Bernardes Ribeiro/CC-BY-SA-3.0, Unknown)

Library of Congress Cataloging-in-Publication Data
Whiting, Jim.
AC Milan / by Jim Whiting.
p. cm. — (Soccer champions)
Includes bibliographical references and index.
Summary: A chronicle of the people, matches,
and world events that shaped the European
men's Italian soccer team known as AC Milan,
from its founding in 1899 to today.
ISBN 978-1-60818-590-0 (hardcover)
ISBN 978-1-62832-195-1 (pbk)
1. Milan (Soccer team)—History. I. Title.

GV943.6.M54W55 2015
796.334'640945211—dc23   2014029641

CCSS: RI.5.1, 2, 3, 8; RH.6-8.4, 5, 7

First Edition HC 9 8 7 6 5 4 3 2 1
First Edition PBK 9 8 7 6 5 4 3 2 1

Cover and page 3: Striker Stephan El Shaarawy
Page 1: A 2013 Serie A match

TABLE OF

Defender Luca Antonini

INTRODUCTION

Soccer (or football, as it is known almost everywhere else in the world) is truly a universal game. Nowhere is the play more competitive than in Europe. Almost every European country has its own league, and generally that league has several divisions. A typical season lasts eight or nine months, from late summer to mid-spring. Every team in each level plays all other teams in its level twice, once at home and once on the other team's pitch. At the end of the season, the bottommost teams in one division are relegated (moved down) to the next lower division, with the same number of topmost teams from that lower division promoted to replace them. Such a system ensures that a high level of competition is maintained and that late-season games between teams with losing records remain important as they seek to avoid relegation.

Individual countries also feature their own tournaments, such as England's FA Cup and Spain's Copa del Rey. In theory, these tournaments allow almost any team the opportunity to win the championship, but in reality the best clubs dominate the competition. An assortment of European-wide tournaments complement individual nations' league and cup play. The most prestigious is the Union of European Football Associations (UEFA) Champions League. Known as the European Cup until

The long, trophy-laden history of Italy's AC Milan has earned the football club legions of devoted fans.

Art.21

16

SODALIVI
ROSSONERO

ACM

OL
STYL
MILAN

99

ANTONIO CON NOI

MILA

1993, the Champions League is a tournament consisting of 32 teams drawn primarily from the highest finishers in the strongest national leagues. Other teams can play their way into the tournament in preliminary rounds. It originated in 1954, when the otherwise obscure Wolverhampton Wanderers of England defeated Honved, the top-rated Hungarian side, prompting Wanderers manager Stan Cullis to declare his team "Champions of the World." Noted French soccer journalist Gabriel Hanot disagreed and helped organize a continent-wide competition that began in 1956.

The Champions League starts with eight four-team pools, which play two games with one another. The top two teams from each pool begin a series of knockout rounds, also contested on a two-game basis. The last two teams play a single championship game at a neutral site. The tournament runs concurrently with league play, beginning in September and concluding in May. Teams that win their league, their national cup, and the Champions League during the same season are said to have won the Continental Treble—certainly the most difficult feat in all of professional sports. The winner of the Champions League is eligible for the FIFA Club World Cup, an annual seven-team tournament that originated in 2000. It also includes teams from the Americas and Caribbean, Africa, Asia, Oceania and the host nation.

The other major European club championship is the UEFA Europa League, founded in 1971 and known as the UEFA Cup until the 2009–10 season. The winners of these two tournaments play for the UEFA Super Cup, usually held in August.

ALL-TIME CHAMPIONS LEAGUE RECORDS OF THE TOP 10 CLUBS (AS OF 2014):

	Winner	Runner-up
Real Madrid (Spain)	10	3
AC Milan (Italy)	7	4
Bayern Munich (Germany)	5	5
Liverpool (England)	5	2
Barcelona (Spain)	4	3
Ajax (Netherlands)	4	2
Manchester United (England)	3	2
Inter Milan (Italy)	3	2
Benfica (Portugal)	2	5
Juventus (Italy)	2	5

Stadio Giuseppe Meazza (San Siro)

CONTINENTAL TREBLE WINNERS

Celtic (Scotland)	1966–67
Ajax (Netherlands)	1971–72
PSV (Netherlands)	1987–88
Manchester United (England)	1998–99
Barcelona (Spain)	2008–09
Inter Milan (Italy)	2009–10
Bayern Munich (Germany)	2012–13

CRICKET AND *CALCIO*

Italy's Benito Mussolini (right) and Germany's Adolf Hitler (left) shared a complex alliance during World War II.

Italy's second-largest city, Milan, is also an old city. Founded nearly 2,500 years ago by a Celtic tribe, it became an important trade center during the Middle Ages. After being ruled by several different countries and kingdoms in the following centuries, it joined a unified Italian nation in 1861. In 1922, Fascist leader Benito Mussolini used Milan as the starting point for his famous March on Rome, a weeklong trek that propelled him to power. Still under Mussolini's direction when World War II began, Italy joined forces with Germany. The city suffered heavy damage from Allied bombing but was quickly rebuilt. Today, it is an important center for fashion, telecommunications, international banking, and automobile manufacturing. Milan is also noted for arts and culture.

Herbert Kilpin's native England was considered the birthplace of soccer.

Visitors throng to the church of Santa Maria delle Grazie to view Leonardo da Vinci's famous painting *The Last Supper*, while opera buffs take their seats at La Scala, perhaps the world's most famous opera theater.

On the pitch, soccer fans throughout the world follow the fortunes of one of the planet's best teams, AC Milan. In 1899, a group of English businessmen living in Milan founded the Milan Cricket and Football Club. The most important figure in the group was Herbert Kilpin, who became the team's first star. He was responsible for choosing the team's distinctive red-and-black-striped shirts. "We are a team of devils," he said. "Our colors are red as fire and black to invoke fear in our opponents." Soon, Milan became known as "Rossoneri" (red and black).

The Rossoneri were so good at scaring their opponents that many early games weren't very competitive. Once, the Milan keeper even brought a chair onto the field. "In the closing stages, he was bored to death," Kilpin said. "He asked me, 'Can't I play a bit as well?' I had him leave the goal, he went up front and scored the 20th goal." Milan won its first trophy, the Medaglia del Re (King's Medal) within a few months of its founding. It also won national championships in 1901, 1906, and 1907. The following year, a group within the club that wanted to include more foreign players broke off and formed a new team: Internazionale Milan, more commonly known as Inter Milan or simply Inter. Whenever the two teams played each other, the match was called the Derby della Madonnina. (In soccer, a "derby" is a rivalry between two teams from the same city or region, while *Madonnina* refers to the statue of the Virgin Mary on top of the Duomo di Milano, or Milan Cathedral.)

In 1909, the Federazione Italiana Football (Italian Football Federation), the national governing body for soccer, changed its name to the Federazione Italiana Giuoco Calcio (FIGC). *Calcio*, which means "kick" in Italian, describes a different, football-like sport but became the official name for modern soccer in Italy. That same year, Piero Pirelli, who had made his fortune from the Pirelli Tire Company, became Milan's team president. He helped provide financial stability for the club.

Soon afterward, Milan acquired Belgian striker Louis Van Hege. In 88 games from 1910 to 1915, Van Hege scored a phenomenal 97 goals before World War I ended his career with Milan. In later life, Van Hege participated on the Olympic stage in 2 sports: soccer in the 1920 and 1924 Summer Games and bobsled in the 1932 Winter Games.

Although the war interrupted soccer at the national championship level from 1914 through 1918, club teams continued to play despite losing players and staff members to the conflict. Championship soccer resumed after the war. Following the 1923–24 season, the winning side had the right to display a *scudetto* (small shield) with the Italian

Duomo di Milano's Madonnina statue is made of gilded copper plates.

national colors on its uniforms, and it became the name of the championship. A Milan star during this era was striker Giuseppe Santagostino, who scored 103 goals between 1921 and 1932.

In 1926, Pirelli footed the bill for what would become the team's longtime home field, Nuovo Stadio Calcistico San Siro (San Siro New Football Stadium), now Stadio Giuseppe Meazza. More commonly referred to as San Siro, after the Milanese district where it is located, the facility has undergone several renovations and currently seats about 80,000 spectators. Milan's first games in its new home were disappointing losses to Inter and league rival Sampierdarenese.

San Siro also serves as the home stadium for Milan's rival Inter, which has won the Scudetto (top) nearly 20 times.

MUSSOLINI MAKES MAJOR MOVES

The year 1926 saw not only a new stadium but also the beginnings of a reorganization of Italian soccer. This was thanks to Mussolini. According to soccer writer Paddy Agnew, Mussolini "quickly realized that sport could provide priceless, positive PR and photo opportunities for him and his regime. He even tried to convince people that the game was not an importation from the dreaded *inglesi* [English] but rather the logical development of the old Florentine calcio."

The new league structure—Serie A at the top, followed by Serie B, and then several Serie C leagues—was in place by 1929. Milan, which had changed its name to Milan Football Club in 1919 to reflect that soccer was now its primary emphasis, finished 11th in Serie A that first season. The team continued to struggle, notching only two third-place finishes by 1941. In 1938, Mussolini ordered the team to change its name again, this time to Associazione Calcio (AC) Milano. (Using the Italian form of the city's name was another way Mussolini tried to distance the sport from its English roots.) The team's best player during this era was striker Aldo Boffi, Serie A's *capocannoniere* (leading goal scorer) in three seasons between 1938 and 1942.

In 187 games from 1936 to 1945 with Milan, Boffi scored 131 goals, ranking him 5th on the team's all-time list as of 2015.

With the end of the war and the death of Mussolini in 1945, Milan underwent its final name change. It now became AC Milan, its English name an homage to its founders. Its fortunes on the pitch began improving, especially after the 1948 Olympics. Milan boosted its roster by signing the three stars of Sweden's gold-medal-winning squad: forward Gunnar Gren, striker Gunnar Nordahl (who would become Milan's all-time leading scorer with 221 goals), and attacking midfielder Nils Liedholm, collectively nicknamed "Gre-No-Li." With the new additions, Milan

In his time as AC Milan coach (1949–52), Lajos Czeizler worked with Nordahl, Gren, and Liedholm (left to right).

Milan's star roster began the 1954–55 season with nine wins and a tie, eventually taking the Serie A championship.

won Serie A in 1950–51, its first national title in more than 40 years. By this time, AC Milan and Inter Milan had been joined by a third Italian powerhouse, Juventus. Between 1950 and 2014, these 3 teams combined to win Serie A 50 times.

AC Milan continued its stellar play during the 1950s, winning the Scudetto again in 1956–57. Liedholm, the longest-serving of the Gre-No-Li trio, departed in 1961, marking the end of an era. A new one arose, though, built around "Golden Boy" midfielder Gianni Rivera. Rivera played a key role in 1963 when Milan defeated the Portuguese club Benfica 2–1 to win its first European Cup. Team captain Cesare Maldini, who had joined the team at the height of the Gre-No-Li era, anchored the defense. Milan took its second European Cup six years later with a 4–1 rout over Ajax, the first team from the Netherlands to advance to the finals. Striker Pierino Prati paced Milan with a hat trick, making him the last of just three men to accomplish the feat in a European Cup/ Champions League final (after Real Madrid's Alfredo Di Stéfano in 1960 and Ferenc Puskás in 1960 and 1962 did so).

After Milan's 10th Serie A title and Rivera's retirement in 1979, the club fell on hard times. It was involved in a match-fixing scandal in 1980 and punished with relegation to Serie B. The Rossoneri immediately won promotion back to Serie A after winning the Serie B title, and then were relegated for 1982–83 because of dismal play. Their record that season of 7 wins, 13 losses, and 10 ties was the worst in team history. Once again, the Rossoneri bounced back, winning Serie B the following year. But the debt-ridden team clearly was in deep trouble, and its president fled the country.

Legendary Gianni Rivera netted 122 times in his 19 seasons with the Rossoneri.

BERLUSCONI BUYS THE TEAM

Six-foot-two Marco Van Basten possessed the power and speed to score as well as the wide vision to assist teammates.

The wealthy Italian media tycoon Silvio Berlusconi bought AC Milan early in 1986 and soon began building a winner. One of his first priorities was to meet with young Dutch striker Marco Van Basten in private. "His secret meeting was to lay the foundation not only for huge sporting success for AC Milan but also, at least partly, for future political triumphs for Mr. Berlusconi," chronicles Paddy Agnew. "Van Basten would prove to be a key element in an impressive array of playing and managerial talent brought together at AC Milan by Berlusconi, talent that very quickly saw the club establish itself as amongst the best in the world."

The following year, Berlusconi signed Van Basten's countryman, Ruud Gullit, whom he described as having "the sun in his heart and dynamite in his muscles." Berlusconi then added a third Dutch star, Frank Rijkaard. Berlusconi's bulging wallet stayed open as he added key Italian players such as midfielder Roberto Donadoni and keeper Giovanni Galli. Berlusconi had also inherited captain Franco Baresi and 17-year-old Paolo Maldini (the son of 1963 European Cup–winning captain Cesare Maldini), who formed the nucleus of a stout defense.

Dutchmen Rijkaard, Van Basten, and Gullit (left to right) comprised one of the most successful trios in soccer history.

Berlusconi knew how to make an impression. He introduced his players to the fans by flying them into the stadium in a helicopter while "Ride of the Valkyries" blared from loudspeakers. The owner was keenly aware of the importance of projecting the "right" image. He ordered his cameramen to focus on happy people in the stands to encourage the idea of attending games as a family activity. He banned fans who flashed signs with racist or anti-Semitic (prejudiced against Jews) messages. He made sure that Van Basten and Gullit promoted an image of racial harmony, even to the point where many fans wore black face paint and false dreadlocks during "Gullit-mania."

The Rossoneri found their rhythm in the late '80s, bringing a host of titles home to Milan.

He also signed obscure coach Arrigo Sacchi, who took a while to gain his players' confidence. When Milan was bounced in the second round of the 1987–88 UEFA Cup by Spain's lightly regarded RCD Espanyol, angry players confronted Sacchi. Berlusconi thundered, "I myself picked Mr. Sacchi, and therefore he will still be here next year. As for all of you, I couldn't be sure."

His persistence—and Sacchi's—paid off. Milan won its first Serie A title of the Berlusconi era in 1987–88 and added the first Supercoppa Italiana, which matched the Serie A and Coppa Italia winners, a few months later. The team appeared in the finals of the European Cup for the first time in 20 years in 1989. Milan's opponents were the Cinderella-story Romanians of FC Steaua Bucureşti, who had knocked off heavily favored FC Barcelona in 1986, thanks to keeper Helmuth Duckadam's stopping four penalty kicks in a shootout. Because of travel restrictions placed on Eastern European teams at the time, UEFA officials feared huge blocks of empty seats. Berlusconi chartered a ship, 25 airplanes, and 450 buses to transport 25,000 fans to Barcelona, the site of the game. This time there would be no fairy godmother watching over the Romanians, who had lost Duckadam to a blood disorder. Gullit and Van Basten each tallied twice in a 4–0 rout.

Milan defended its title the following year against Benfica. Frustrated for much of the match, Milan finally broke through in the 68th minute. Van Basten flicked the ball to Rijkaard, who outran two defenders and launched the game-winner from the midway point of the penalty area.

While the "Dutch Treat" garnered most of the headlines during this era, the equally important but less flashy defenders Maldini, Baresi, Alessandro Costacurta, and Mauro Tassotti got the job done. Maldini said, "Defenders receive less attention from fans than goal-scorers. We are more in the engine room."

If Milan's defenders were doing the grunt work of the ship, then Berlusconi was its captain on the bridge. He loved being in the spotlight and never missed an opportunity to remind people of what he had brought to the team. In 1991, he told *Gazzetta dello Sport*, "I don't want to play down the contributions made by anyone else, but my presence as AC Milan president over the last four years has been, at the very least, very important if not absolutely critical." Berlusconi had plenty of reasons to be proud of the club's success since 1986, a period during which the Rossoneri clinched a Scudetto, the two European Cups, and five other major trophies.

Future Italian Football Hall of Famer Baresi celebrated Milan's 1989 European Cup win.

THE INVINCIBLES

When Milan's 1990–91 season ended with a 0–0 tie against Parma and a runner-up finish in Serie A, few people paid attention. But it was the start of a still-record Serie A 58-game unbeaten streak that extended to March 1993 and included 2 league titles. The Italian sports press nicknamed Milan "Gli Invicibili" (The Invincibles). The team made it three titles in a row in 1993–94, allowing just 15 goals while scoring 36. Manager Fabio Capello soon discovered the fickle nature of fandom, though. After Roberto Baggio, the 1993 FIFA World Player of the Year, joined Milan, Capello took the team to another Scudetto in 1995–96.

Then he coached Spanish powerhouse Real Madrid to a league title the following year. Capello returned to Milan for the 1997–98 season and was roundly booed (and quickly fired) after the Rossoneri stumbled to a 10th-place Serie A finish.

The European Cup changed both its name and its format in 1993. Milan reached the finals of what was now the "Champions League" as a heavy favorite over the French side Olympic Marseille, having won every game leading to the final and yielding just a single goal. Milan forward Daniele Massaro nearly scored twice early on, but his header went wide, and Marseille

Striker Jean-Pierre Papin took on his former Marseille team during the hotly contested 1993 European Cup final.

keeper Fabien Barthez punched away his volley from nearly point-blank range. Just before halftime, Marseille defender Basile Boli soared high into the air for a corner kick and headed the ball into the net. Milan couldn't respond, and in a shocking upset, Marseille became the first French team to win the title.

Milan won its third consecutive Serie A championship in 1993–94 before capturing the Champions League trophy.

In another startling upset the next year, Milan—this time the underdog—turned the tables on Barcelona in a surprisingly easy 4–0 romp. Milan took on the Dutch squad AFC Ajax in the 1995 Champions League final, with hopes of tying Real Madrid's total of six cups. Frank Rijkaard, now with Ajax, did everything he could to thwart his former team. His perfect pass through a pair of Milan defenders into the penalty area in the 85th minute allowed 18-year-old Ajax striker Patrick Kluivert to become the youngest player to score a goal in the finals. That goal won the game. "It was incredible because we did it with a lot of youngsters against a well-experienced team," Rijkaard said.

Led by Paolo Maldini (with trophy), Milan was victorious against Juventus in the first all-Italian Champions League final in 2003.

After another Scudetto in 1998–99, Milan entered a relative dry spell, with no titles for three years. The bright spot was the 1999 debut of Andriy Shevchenko, a Ukrainian striker who would go on to lead the team in scoring for 6 of his 7 years and whose 175 career goals ranked second to Nordahl's in team records.

The club ascended to the summit of European soccer again in 2003, defeating Juventus in the Champions League final on penalty kicks. The win came on the 40th anniversary of Milan's first triumph in the competition. Team captain Maldini followed in his father's footsteps, making history as the third father-son duo to have captained winning teams. Milan also enjoyed a rare win in the Coppa Italia—just

Kaká (#22) battled against defenders such as Juárez Teixeira (#39) of Italy's AC Siena.

its fifth ever and first since 1977. A third-place finish in Serie A kept Milan from being the first Italian team to win the Continental Treble, though.

A key addition came in the 2003–04 season, when future Brazilian superstar Kaká joined the team. Milan won both the Scudetto and the UEFA Super Cup, while Kaká's first season with the Rossoneri was good enough for him to finish ninth in balloting for FIFA World Player of the Year.

The team looked to add its seventh European Cup against Liverpool in 2005, the 50th anniversary of the competition. Maldini, now 38 and still playing at the top of his game, became the oldest player to score in the Cup final when he volleyed home a pass in the opening moments. Striker Hernán Crespo added two more scores just before halftime for a seemingly invincible 3–0 lead. But in what Liverpool fans term "the Miracle of Istanbul" [the site of the match], their side scored three times in a six-minute span in the second half and won on penalty kicks.

ON TOP OF THE WORLD

Inzaghi, Kaká, and defender Marek Jankulovski each tallied once to put Milan on top in the 2007 UEFA Super Cup.

Milan took its seventh Champions League title in 2007, reversing the outcome of the Liverpool "miracle" two years earlier. Buoyed by the win, the Rossoneri kept adding to their trophy collection that year. Three months later, they defeated Sevilla 3–1 in the UEFA Super Cup. It was the fifth time they had hoisted the cup, more than any other team. Four months later, Milan became the first European team to win the FIFA Club World Cup. The Rossoneri defeated the Urawa Red Diamonds of host

After six years with Milan, superstar Kaká left in 2009 to join Spain's Real Madrid for a transfer fee of about $92 million.

Japan in the semifinals, with midfielder Clarence Seedorf scoring the game's only goal midway through the second half. Three days later, they broke a 1–1 tie with the Argentine Boca Juniors as forward Filippo Inzaghi scored twice in the 4–2 victory. To many soccer authorities, that victory secured Milan's standing as the world's most successful club team. Its 18 international trophies were the most of any club—until Boca Juniors matched the achievement the following year.

Milan's success was not limited to the international scene. Starting with the 2008–09 season, Milan placed in the top three in Serie A for the next five years, which included winning the Scudetto in 2010–11. A notable addition to the roster during this time was the iconic midfielder David Beckham, who played parts of 2008–09 and 2009–10 during his breaks from American Major League Soccer. At first, many Milanese doubted Beckham's value, believing that his addition was a marketing stunt. But Beckham quickly won them over. After a 1–1 tie in which Beckham scored the Milan goal, the newspaper *Gazzetta dello Sport* said, "If all Milan's players battled like he does, they would not be looking up at Inter and Juventus."

However, Beckham was long gone by the 2013–14 season, when the bottom fell out. Several key players retired, and two more were sold before league play began. Milan finished eighth in Serie A, bowed out of the Coppa Italia in the quarterfinals—dropping a 2–1 home decision to Udinese Calcio, a team that had won just a handful of trophies in its long existence—and lost in the quarterfinals of the Champions League. The 2014–15 season would be the first since 1998–99 that

David Beckham brought his infamous crosses and free kicks to Milan's midfield.

5. 00

FORZA MILAN

UVE TI ODIO

KAKÀ

BALO IS BACK!

GRAZIE A DIO

NON SONO GOBBO

the Rossoneri didn't figure in the ranks of European competition.

This downturn was not expected to last long, though. Former player Filippo Inzaghi took over coaching duties and was described by Berlusconi as "hungry for victory." Milan looked to forward Stephan El Shaarawy for leadership on the field. Nicknamed "Il Faraone" (The Pharaoh) because of his Egyptian heritage, he had been Milan's youngest-ever goal scorer in the Champions League. Experienced goalkeeper Diego López joined the Rossoneri in 2014 and began to find his stride. The team also looked to build with youth, as evidenced by 15-year-old forward Hachim Mastour's inclusion in the final game of the 2013–14 season. "It is impossible to take the ball from Hachim," said Mastour's Under-17 coach, Omar Danesi. "For the talent he has, he is definitely a player to play at the San Siro [for Milan]."

Twice during the Roman era, Italy was governed by a triumvirate—a group of three rulers. Today's Italian triumvirate is composed of soccer teams instead. Alongside Inter Milan and Juventus, AC Milan is justly proud of its heritage as one prong of Italy's soccer elite, and it looks to maintain that lofty position for many years to come.

AC Milan fans remain as dedicated as ever as they wait for their next championship.

MEMORABLE MATCHES

1899

Team was founded.

1949

AC Milan v. Inter Milan
Derby della Madonnina, November 6, 1949, Milan, Italy

When Milan met Inter in November 1949, fans expected to witness a high-scoring match. Even so, they could not have foreseen what followed. Milan jumped in front when winger Enrico Candiani punched in two quick goals. Following an Inter score, striker Gunnar Nordahl scored at 14 minutes, and midfielder Nils Liedholm extended the Milan lead 5 minutes later to 4–1. But two Inter goals within a minute of each other late in the first half gave those fans hope. Inter maintained the momentum with two more goals early in the second half to take the lead. After midfielder Carlo Annovazzi knotted the score at 5–5, Inter's Amadeo Amadei scored his third goal of the match—just one of four hat tricks in Derby history. The rest of the game remained scoreless. Inter keeper Angelo Franzosi saved a shot by forward Gunnar Gren that looked as though it had crossed the line, and in the waning moments, Candiani narrowly missed a hat trick of his own when his blast caromed off the crossbar. The 11 total goals are a Derby mark that is unlikely to be broken.

1963

AC Milan v. Benfica

European Cup Final, May 22, 1963, London, England

Five years after its first appearance in a European Cup final, Milan took on two-time winner Benfica. One of the key Milan newcomers was 19-year-old midfielder Gianni Rivera, dubbed "the wonder boy of Italian football." According to Europeancuphistory.com, "He was the creative heart of the side, particularly in his understanding with [striker José] Altafini ahead of him, and this relationship would prove particularly fruitful when it most mattered." Benfica's star forward Eusébio opened the scoring 19 minutes into the match. But Milan had an answer ready in Altafini, who had scored an astonishing eight goals against US Luxembourg in the opening round of the tournament. With Rivera assisting, Altafini fired from inside the penalty area 13 minutes into the second half to tie the score. About 10 minutes later, Rivera sent a perfect pass to the onrushing striker, and Altafini easily beat Benfica keeper Costa Pereira. The Portuguese wanted an offside call but didn't get it. Milan's 2–1 victory that day brought the European Cup to Italy for the first time. It was the country's first international success since winning the World Cup 25 years earlier.

1973

AC Milan v. Hellas Verona

Serie A Match, May 20, 1973, Verona, Italy

A few days after capturing the Winners' Cup (a tournament matching the winners of all European competitions) with a 1–0 victory over Leeds, Milan anticipated adding the Serie A title to its collection. In the season's final game at Verona, the Rossoneri faced a team that had spent most of its existence in Serie B and was again on the verge of relegation. Their seemingly hapless rivals hadn't scored more than twice in a game all season. Surprisingly, Verona took a 3–1 lead in the first half and coasted to a 5–3 upset victory. The loss dropped Milan into second behind Juventus, depriving it of a 10th Scudetto. In 1990, history seemed to repeat itself, as a 2–1 loss at Verona in the season's next-to-last game cost Milan the Serie A title. Memories of key losses to "Fatal Verona" continue to haunt Milan when it visits Bentegodi Stadium. The PA system blares, "Milanisti! Welcome to the fatal Verona." The crowd chants, "*Quanti scudetti avete voi ...*" (How many championships do you have ...). Then it answers: "*Due di meno, due di meno ...*" (Two less, two less ...).

1994

AC Milan v. FC Barcelona

Champions League Final, May 18, 1994, Athens, Greece

AC Milan tried not to panic as it prepared for the 1994 Champions League final against Spanish La Liga champion Barcelona. Several key players were either injured or suspended, while others were barred from playing because UEFA rules limited teams to three non-nationals. Despite these handicaps, Milan dominated the match. Forward Daniele Massaro converted a cross from a tight angle in the 22nd minute. He poked in his second goal from 18 yards out just before halftime after a long run by midfielder/winger Dejan Savićević. Moments into the second half, Savićević capitalized on a defensive error and lobbed a perfect ball over the keeper's head from the left side of the penalty area. Ten minutes later, defensive midfielder Marcel Desailly curved a ball around the onrushing keeper from about 15 yards out. Many soccer experts described Milan's win as the most dominating performance in Cup history. Desailly added a bit of history of his own. The previous year, he had played for the winning Marseille team, so he became the first player to win the Cup with two different teams in consecutive seasons.

2003

AC Milan v. Juventus

Champions League Final, May 28, 2003, Manchester, England

In 2003, two of the most dominant European club soccer teams met in the first all-Italian finals at perhaps the sport's most hallowed pitch—Old Trafford in Manchester, England. Juventus entered as Italian champions for the 27th time, while Milan had had to scramble to even qualify for the Cup. In a sport often known for feuding and fighting, this match was a notable exception. According to German referee Markus Merk, the game was "the highlight of my career because the atmosphere was so positive and fair." An apparent early goal by Milan striker Andriy Shevchenko was declared offside, while Juventus's Antonio Conte's late header caromed off the goalpost. The scoreless match then went to penalty kicks. Each team made just one of its first three tries. After Juventus missed its fourth, center-back Alessandro Nesta put Milan ahead. Juventus drew even on its fifth shot. But Shevchenko calmly rolled the ball into the right side of the net, while Juventus keeper Gianluigi Buffon tumbled in the wrong direction. The triumph gave Milan its sixth cup, putting it behind only Real Madrid of Spain.

2007

AC Milan v. Liverpool

Champions League Final, May 23, 2007, Athens, Greece

Two years earlier, Milan had been on the wrong side of "the Miracle of Istanbul," squandering a three-goal halftime lead to Liverpool in the final and losing on penalty kicks. The 2007 rematch almost never happened. Milan was one of several clubs involved in a match-fixing scandal in 2006 and had to win a qualifying game simply to get into the tournament. Once in, Milan survived two losses in the group stage before defeating Celtic (Scotland) in the round of 16 and Bayern Munich and Manchester United in subsequent rounds to reach the finals. Milan caught a huge break in the first half when a free kick rebounded off striker Filippo Inzaghi's arm. Liverpool keeper Pepe Reina lunged toward the ball's original path, but Inzaghi's accidental deflection sent the ball into the net. Inzaghi extended the lead with eight minutes remaining. He took a perfect pass from Kaká, sprinted down the center of the field, and then rolled the ball under Reina's outstretched arms into the net. A Liverpool goal with fewer than two minutes remaining raised hopes for another miracle, but time ran out.

FAMOUS FOOTBALLERS

HERBERT KILPIN

(1870–1916)
Player/manager, 1899–1908

Born in the English city of Nottingham, Kilpin began playing soccer seriously in his early teens. His team was named for the famous 19th-century Italian nationalist Giuseppe Garibaldi. Garibaldi and his followers wore red shirts, and Kilpin's English team imitated them. Kilpin moved to Torino, Italy, in the early 1890s to further his career in textiles. He became the first-ever Englishman to play soccer abroad when he joined a team there. He maintained his enthusiasm for the game after moving to Milan and cofounding the Milan Cricket and Football Club. As player/manager, he helped the team to national titles in 1901, 1906, and 1907. He died in poverty in 1916 and was buried in an unmarked grave. AC Milan fan Luigi La Rocca found Kilpin's grave in the 1990s and encouraged the team to pay for a new headstone. Kilpin was reburied in the Monumental Graveyard in Milan, the final resting place for the city's most illustrious citizens. Despite his enduring fame, records indicate that he played in only 27 games during his stint with the club, scoring 7 goals.

SILVIO BERLUSCONI

(1936–)
Owner, 1986–present

Silvio Berlusconi was always a businessman: in elementary school, he did others' homework assignments in exchange for snacks. He formed a band that played on cruise ships when he was in high school. Eventually, he built Italy's largest media empire, which made him the nation's wealthiest man. After buying AC Milan in 1986, he spent freely to assemble top talent and drew on his media experience to promote the team—and himself. "Where there was Milan success, there was the broadly smiling face of *padrone* [patron] Berlusconi, either standing proudly over the latest piece of heavyweight silverware won by the team or being thrown in the air by his jubilant players," says soccer writer Paddy Agnew. In 1994, Berlusconi made use of his team's high profile when he entered politics. He even borrowed a phrase from soccer when he announced his bid for Parliament, saying (in Italian), "I have chosen to take to the field." He won the election and was named Italian prime minister. During his political career, Berlusconi has been frequently investigated for alleged criminal activities, but many Italians still think highly of him.

GIANNI RIVERA

(1943–)
Midfielder, 1960–79

Gianni Rivera's extraordinary soccer skills became apparent at a young age. He made his Serie A debut for his hometown Alessandria team at the age of 15. Milan paid a then record $200,000 transfer fee to acquire him. The most dominant European midfielder of his time, in 1969, he became the first Italian to win the coveted Ballon d'Or. A year later, English national team coach Alf Ramsey was asked to name the four best Italian players. "Rivera, Rivera, Rivera, Rivera," he replied. By the time Rivera retired in 1979, he could boast of three Serie A titles and a pair of European Cups. As of 2015, he ranked third on Milan's all-time scoring list with 164 goals. As soccer writer John Foot notes, "The rule was simple—pass to Rivera, give him the ball…. Rivera's specialty was the final ball, the most difficult and delicate art in football." In 1998, an international panel of judges named him the greatest Italian soccer player ever. In his later years, Rivera was elected to the Italian Parliament and then served as a member of the European Union Parliament.

MARCO VAN BASTEN

(1964–)
Striker, 1987-95

After a stellar six-year career with Ajax in which he averaged almost a goal per match, Marco Van Basten was Silvio Berlusconi's first major acquisition. Nicknamed the "Swan of Utrecht" for his elegant looks and Netherlandish home, he won the prestigious Ballon d'Or three times while with Milan. Soon after becoming the first player to score four goals during a Champions League game in 1992, Van Basten severely injured his ankle. He had to retire two years later. The English publication *Sky Sports* ranked him number one among great athletes whose careers were cut short by injury. As teammate Paolo Maldini said, "The only downside is that he retired too soon. That was a shame, not just for AC Milan fans, but for all lovers of good football. He stopped at the peak of his career, but nevertheless he did things that no other player I've played with could do." Van Basten enjoyed deep respect among his countrymen. A 2004 poll placed him 25th among the 100 greatest Dutch people of all time.

PAOLO MALDINI

(1968–)
Defender, 1985-2009

Though Paolo Maldini was born too late to watch his father Cesare play, he clearly inherited his father's talent. Many soccer experts believe that Cesare and Paolo are the greatest father-son tandem in European soccer history. Paolo played more than 900 games during his 24-season Milan career, virtually all of them at the sport's highest levels. In 1995, he nearly became the first defender to win the FIFA World Player of the Year award, finishing second in the voting. Twelve years later, at the age of 39, he was named Champions League Best Defender. "Maldini was a unique footballer, part of a select band of players that believe loyalty and respect transcend money and materialism," noted *Forza Italian Football*. "A player of class, grace, substance, and style, there are very few Paolo Maldinis in world football." Maldini's jersey number 3 was retired after his final game in 2009, but that retirement may be only temporary. One of Maldini's sons, Christian or Daniel, might have the opportunity to wear it someday. Both boys were playing in the AC Milan youth system as of 2015.

KAKÁ

(1982–)
Attacking midfielder, 2003-09, 2013-14

Ricardo Izecson dos Santos Leite was known as "Kaká" from the time his younger brother could talk. After a swimming pool accident broke a bone in his back at the age of 18, Kaká recovered in time to make the 2002 World Cup–winning Brazilian team. He joined AC Milan in 2003 and reached the summit of his sport in 2007 when he was named FIFA World Player of the Year. The following year, *TIME* magazine named him among the 100 most influential people in the world. "He's an attacking midfielder with tremendous technical ability and great size and is good in the air," said American goalkeeper—and frequent opponent—Kasey Keller. "He is the total footballer." Kaká was also known for his work as an ambassador with the United Nations World Food Program. A man of strong Christian beliefs, he expressed interest in becoming a minister when his playing days end. Fans follow his every move on Twitter—where he became the first athlete to amass more than 10 million followers. Unfortunately for the Milan faithful, Kaká ended his contract in 2014.

AC MILAN TITLES
THROUGH 2014

**EUROPEAN CUP/
CHAMPIONS
LEAGUE**

Winner
1963
1969
1989
1990
1994
2003
2007
Total: 7

Runner-up
1958
1993
1995
2005
Total: 4

COPPA ITALIA

1967
1972
1973
1977
2003
Total: 5

SERIE A

1950–51
1954–55
1956–57
1958–59
1961–62
1967–68
1978–79
1987–88
1991–92
1992–93
1993–94
1995–96
1998–99
2003–04
2010–11
Total: 15

SUPER CUP

1989
1990
1994
2003
2007
Total: 5

SELECTED BIBLIOGRAPHY

Agnew, Paddy. *Forza Italia: The Fall and Rise of Italian Football*. London: Ebury, 2007.

Foot, John. *Winning at All Costs: A Scandalous History of Italian Soccer*. New York: Nation Books, 2007.

Goldblatt, David, and Johnny Acton. *The Soccer Book: The Sport, the Teams, the Tactics, the Cups*. New York: DK, 2010.

UEFA. *Champions of Europe, 1955–2005: 50 Years of the World's Greatest Club Football; The Best Goals from All 50 Finals*. DVD. Pleasanton, Calif.: Soccer Learning Systems, 2005.

WEBSITES

AC MILAN
http://www.acmilan.com/en
AC Milan official website. Includes team history, current and past
seasons, photos, continually updated news, and more.

PLANET MILAN
http://www.planetmilan.com/index.html
AC Milan website with news, match previews and reviews, information and
goals, team history, notable players, championship teams, and more.

Note: Every effort has been made to ensure that the websites listed above are suitable
for children, that they have educational value, and that they contain no inappropriate
material. However, because of the nature of the Internet, it is impossible to guarantee that
these sites will remain active indefinitely or that their contents will not be altered.

INDEX